For Mary Swope —S.M.S.

For my mom, Joyce —E.J.B.

Farrar, Straus and Giroux New York

THE KRAZEES

Story by
SAM SWOPE

Pictures by
ERiC BrACE

Do you ever feel like Iggie
when the rain goes plipple plop?
All day long, just plipple plopple
plipple plopple dipple dop?

And each plipple and each plopple
makes you feel all bungleboo?

Plipple plopple plopple plipple
and you don't know what to do?

Do you ever get the Krazees?
Do they make your razzle tig?
Do they frazzle your bombazzle
till you shilly up your shig?

Do they biggle your bumdiggle?
Do they make you wiggle red?

Do you ever feel like Iggie,
getting Krazees in your head?

Have you ever seen the Krazees?

Have you seen them here and there?

Have you seen them in your TV set
and in your underwear?

Have you seen them in the bathroom,
where they stiggle up the sink,
where they squiggle and they squaggle
like a rumple dumple dink?

Have you seen them in the kitchen,
where they gumble up the food?

Who can stop the crazy Krazees
when they're in a crazy mood!

They will bimble bop wherever!
They will ingle dingle dop!

They will oodle noodle doodle
till the willy wingles pop!

Oh, those Krazees make you crazy!

Bad bad Krazees

BOOM BOOM BOOM!

Now, you cut that out, you Krazees—

Oops, there goes the living room.

Then plipple plop bim bango—poof!

Those Krazees go away.

Did you ever say like Iggie,

"I've had such a Krazee Day!"

And who can tell what happened—
What makes Krazees come and go?
You can giggle till the pig'll crow
and still you will not know.
Oh, well.

Do you ever feel like Iggie
when the sun is shining bright?

Jumping stomping bongo bopping,

not a Krazee left in sight?

Color separations by Hong Kong Scanner Arts
Printed and bound in the United States of America by Berryville Graphics. Designed by Filomena Tuosto
First edition, 1997

Library of Congress Cataloging-in-Publication Data
Swope, Sam.
The Krazees / story by Sam Swope ; pictures by Eric Brace.
p.   cm.
Summary: Describes the havoc created when "The Krazees" take over Iggie's house and head on a boring rainy day.
ISBN 0-374-34281-4
[1. Stories in rhyme.   2. Humorous stories.]   I. Brace, Eric, ill.   II. Title.
PZ8.3.S9957Kr   1997   [E]—DC20   92-24435